The Reactions of Metals

Roberta Baxter

Raintree

Chicago, Illinois

© 2009 Raintree
a division of Pearson Inc.
Chicago, Illinois

Customer Service 888-454-2279
Visit our website at www.heinemannraintree.com

Editorial: Megan Cotugno and Andrew Farrow
Design: Philippa Jenkins
Illustrations: KJA-artists.com
Picture Research: Ruth Blair
Production: Alison Parsons
Originated by Modern Age
Printed and bound in China by Leo Paper Group

13 12 11 10 09
10 9 8 7 6 5 4 3 2 1

Library of Congress Cataloging-in-Publication Data
Baxter, Roberta, 1952-
 The reactions of metals / Roberta Baxter.
   p. cm. -- (Sci-hi. Physical science)
 Includes bibliographical references and index.
 ISBN 978-1-4109-3246-4 (hc) -- ISBN 978-1-4109-3261-7 (pb) 1. Metals. 2. Chemical reactions. I. Title.
 QD171.B33 2008
 546'.3--dc22

                              2008026148

Acknowledgments
The author and publishers are grateful to the following for permission to reproduce copyright material: © Advertising Archives p. **27**; © Alamy/Bill Bachman p. **34**; © Alamy/Danita Delimont p. **25**; © Alamy/Diane Randell p. **24**; © Alamy/ImageState p. **30**; © Alamy/Phil Degginger p. **41** (bottom); © Alamy/Stockfolio p. **37**; © Alamy/Visual Arts Library (London) p. **5**; © Alamy/Florida Images p. **20**; © Alamy/Peter Barritt p. **32**; © Corbis/Heinz Mollenhauer/Zefa p. **23**; © Getty Images/Photographer's Choice p. **7**; © John Pucek p. **39**; © NASA/Jim Grossmann p. **41** (top); © PA Photos/AP/Achmad Ibrahim p. **35**; © Photodisc/McDaniel Woolf p. **iii** (Contents), **21**; © Science Photo Library/A. Cornu, Publiphoto Diffusion p. **9**; © Science Photo Library/Andrew Lambert Photography p. **11** (top); © Science Photo Library/Charles D. Winters pp. **12**, **16**, **17**, **26**; © Science Photo Library/Colin Cuthbert p. **18**; © Science Photo Library/Jerry Mason p. **11** (bottom); © Science Photo Library/Los Almos National Laboratory p. **17**; © Science Photo Library/Martyn F. Chillmaid p. **14**; © Science Photo Library/Pascal Goetgheluck p. **33**; © Science Photo Library/Sam Ogden p. **19**; © Science Photo Library/Sheila Terry p. **28**; © Science Photo Library/U.S. Dept. of Energy p. **6**; © Shutterstock p. **36**; background images and design features throughout.

Cover photographs reproduced with permission of © Corbis/Lucidio Studio Inc. **main**; © Getty Images/Photographer's Choice **inset**.

The publishers would like to thank literacy consultant Nancy Harris and content consultant Dr. Ted Dolter for their assistance in the preparation of this book.

Every effort has been made to contact copyright holders of any material reproduced in this book. Any omissions will be rectified in subsequent printings if notice is given to the publisher.

Some words are shown in bold, **like this**. These words are explained in the glossary. You will find important information and definitions underlined and in bold, **like this**.

Contents

Can you clean the Statue of Liberty? Go to page 21 to see.

What metal is good for mending a broken bone? Find out on page 39!

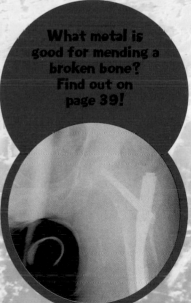

Metals Are All Around Us

Metals are all around us. They support buildings and are used to make cars and planes. Metals can carry electricity and are found in utensils such as spoons and knives. Metals also react with other substances to produce important chemicals.

The properties of metals

What are metals like? Most metals:

• are shiny
• **conduct** electricity
• conduct heat
• can be bent and squeezed into new shapes
• can react with other chemicals

Today, scientists understand lots of things about metals. They use this knowledge to make tools and machines. They also know how metals can be used to make new substances.

Metals in history

People have recognized the value of metals since ancient times. Learning to work metals was an important advance for ancient humans. Historians give a name to the time: the Bronze Age. This was when humans learned to refine (remove impurities from) copper and tin. They melted the copper and tin together to create a stronger metal called bronze. With that technology, humans could make better tools and weapons.

Later, humans learned to build very hot fires, called furnaces. They began to forge iron by heating and beating it. Historians call this time the Iron Age. Iron was cheaper and easier to obtain than the tin and copper used for bronze. So most tools and weapons were made from iron.

Ancient humans used bronze to make weapons.

How many metals can you name?

How many do you think there are?

Particles in metal

All metals are made up of tiny particles called atoms.
Atoms are not all alike. An iron atom is different from a gold
atom. Each kind of atom is a different **element** such as gold.

Many metals

About three-fourths of the 118 elements are metals. Some
of these metals are hard, shiny materials, like the metals we
have in our homes. Sodium and potassium are shiny metals.
They can react so easily with air and water that they must
be kept under oil. Other metals might not seem like metals
at all.

Plutonium glows
because it is
radioactive.

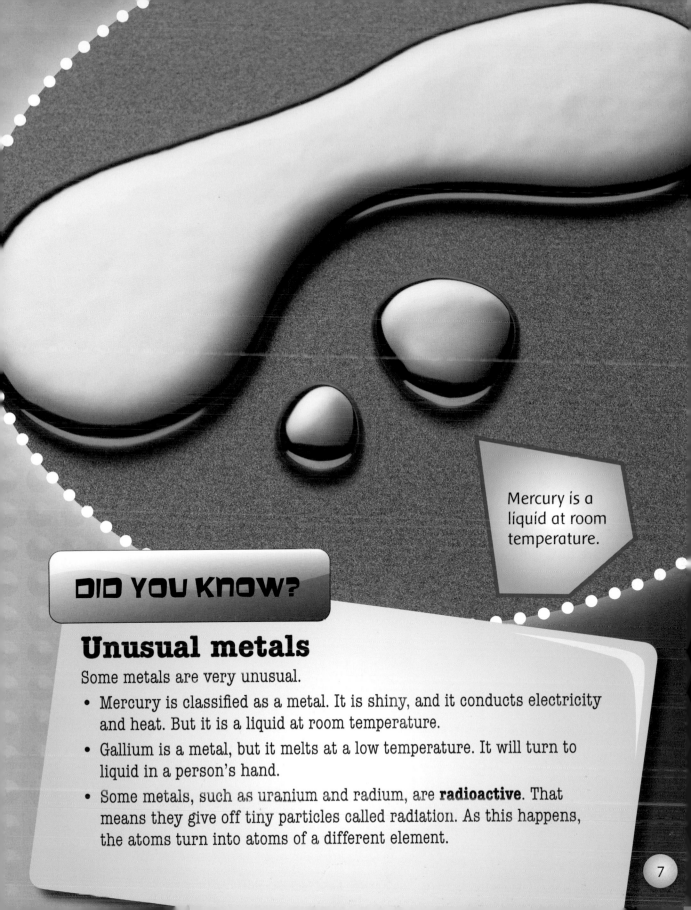

Mercury is a liquid at room temperature.

Unusual metals

Some metals are very unusual.

- Mercury is classified as a metal. It is shiny, and it conducts electricity and heat. But it is a liquid at room temperature.

- Gallium is a metal, but it melts at a low temperature. It will turn to liquid in a person's hand.

- Some metals, such as uranium and radium, are **radioactive**. That means they give off tiny particles called radiation. As this happens, the atoms turn into atoms of a different element.

Metals React

Metals can react (combine) with other atoms to make other substances, called **compounds**. <u>**A compound is a substance made of two or more elements combined together.**</u>

A compound usually has different properties than the atoms from which it was made. Some metals, such as potassium and sodium, react easily to form compounds. Other metals, such as gold, hardly react at all.

Reactive metals?

Scientists have set up a chart telling what metals are more active than others. It is called the **activity series**. Potassium is the most reactive metal. Aluminum and iron are in the middle, and gold is the least reactive. By using this chart, scientists can predict how likely metals are to react with other substances.

Activity Series

React more easily

potassium

sodium

calcium

magnesium

aluminum

zinc

iron

tin

lead

(hydrogen)

copper

silver

platinum

gold

React less easily

The activity series shows that gold, platinum, and silver do not react easily. For this reason, all three are used to make jewelry, because they stay shiny and do not change into other substances!

Gold is not dissolved by most acids, even strong ones.

9

Formula equations

Throughout this book, you will see equations with chemical symbols instead of words. The symbol for each element is shown in the **periodic table of elements** (shown below).

An equation that uses symbols is called a **formula equation**. You will see one on the opposite page. It is read just like a word equation. The plus sign means "reacts with" and the arrow sign means "produces."

To make formula equations more useful, **coefficients** are added to balance the equation. Coefficients are the numbers placed in front of the chemical symbols. They show that the same number of each kind of atom will enter and leave a reaction.

The Periodic Table

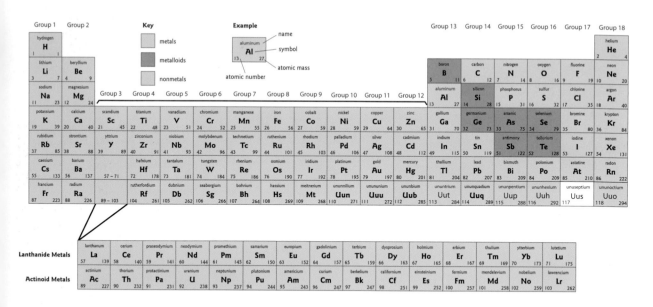

Metals are represented in green in this periodic table. You will learn more reactions of metals throughout this book.

Reactions with water

Some metals react with water. For example, sodium reacts with water to produce hydrogen gas and a compound called sodium hydroxide. Scientists write the equation as follows:

$$2Na + 2H_2O \rightarrow 2NaOH + H_2$$

sodium + water → sodium hydroxide + hydrogen (gas)

The gas can be collected in a flask. When a burning splint is put into the flask, a popping sound will happen. The pop shows that the gas is hydrogen, burning quickly.

A lot of heat is produced when sodium and potassium react with water. The heat can make the hydrogen gas start to burn during the reaction. The flame will be violet when potassium reacts with water. It will be yellow when sodium reacts with water.

Hydroxide ions

These reactions produce substances called hydroxide ions—this is the OH in the equation above. If there are lots of hydroxide ions, that makes the substance a strong **base**. **A base is a compound that accepts a hydrogen ion in a chemical reaction.** This is the opposite of an **acid**, which releases a hydrogen ion. Bases are used as drain cleaners and to make soap. Strong bases can burn your skin, so you must take special care when handling them.

Potassium reacts with water. It forms potassium hydroxide and hydrogen gas.

See the yellow flame color that is produced when sodium reacts with water?

Reactions with acids

Some metals react with acids. Most metals, such as sodium and potassium, react more violently with acid than they react with water.

When sodium is mixed with hydrochloric acid, the reaction produces sodium chloride. Sodium chloride is what we know as table salt. **All reactions of metals with acids produce a compound called a salt.** The reaction also produces hydrogen gas and a lot of heat.

$$2Na + 2HCl \rightarrow 2NaCl + H_2$$

sodium + hydrochloric → sodium + hydrogen
acid   chloride (salt)   (gas)

Metals lower down on the activity series do not react as easily as sodium and potassium. If a metal is above hydrogen on the activity chart, it can react with acids. Tin put in some **dilute** acid will begin to produce some bubbles, showing that a reaction is taking place. The reaction produces hydrogen gas and a salt.

Tin reacts with acid, releasing bubbles of hydrogen.

The King of Metals

Gold, considered the "king of metals," can only be dissolved in a reaction with a mixture of concentrated nitric acid and hydrochloric acid. This mixture is called "aqua regia," royal water, meaning that it dissolves. The word *regia* comes from a word for king, like the word regal. In ancient times, if a metal dissolved when a drop of acid was placed on it, that meant it was not real gold. Only gold could withstand most acids.

More reactions with acids

Copper, silver, and gold are lower than hydrogen in the activity series. They will not react in dilute acids (acids in a lot of water). They only react in concentrated acids (acids in a little water).

- Copper will react in strong nitric acid.

- Silver requires **concentrated** acid to react.

Acid-base reactions

You have just learned that metals can react with water to form bases. These bases can react with acids. **The reaction between an acid and a base is called neutralization.**

The products of this reaction are a salt and water. For example, hydrochloric acid reacts with sodium hydroxide (a base) to form sodium chloride and water. Sodium chloride is what we call table salt.

$$HCl + NaOH \rightarrow NaCl + H_2O$$

hydrochloric + sodium → sodium + water
acid   hydroxide   chloride
             (base)   (salt)

How do we know that a salt is formed? If the water is boiled off, a solid remains. The solid is a salt.

Salt remains after water is boiled completely.

More reactions between acids and bases

Other acids and bases that come from metals react in a similar way. When sulfuric acid and potassium hydroxide react, the product is another salt, potassium sulfate.

$$H_2SO_4 + 2KOH \rightarrow K_2SO_4 + 2H_2O$$

sulfuric acid + potassium → potassium + water
hydroxide sulfate
(base) (a salt)

If you see this, it's a salt!

If you see these names in a chemical compound, the compound is a salt.

NAMES	EXAMPLES
chloride	sodium chloride ($NaCl$)
sulfide	potassium sulfide (K_2S)
carbonate	calcium carbonate ($CaCO_3$)
sulfate	zinc sulfate ($ZnSO_4$)
nitrate	silver nitrate ($AgNO_3$)
phosphate	sodium phosphate (Na_3PO_4)
nitrite	potassium nitrite (KNO_2)
cyanide	lithium cyanide ($LiCN$)

Displacement Reactions

The **activity series** is important in predicting an important class of reactions. **In a displacement reaction, one element displaces another.** This means they switch places.

For example, zinc displaces copper in this reaction:

$$CuSO_4 + Zn \rightarrow ZnSO_4 + Cu$$

copper sulfate + zinc → zinc sulfate + copper

This reaction takes place because zinc is above copper in the activity series. The reaction would not work the other way round. Copper will not displace zinc.

Can you see the reaction between zinc and copper taking place?

Can you see the reaction between copper and silver nitrate?

Look again at the activity series. Do you think copper will displace silver in a reaction?

$$2AgNO_3 + Cu \rightarrow Cu(NO_3)_2 + 2Ag$$
silver nitrate + copper → copper nitrate + silver

Yes, copper displaces silver in the reaction above. The silver nitrate is **dissolved** in water, and everything looks clear. But as the copper displaces the silver, the silver appears as a solid. A solid formed like this is called a **precipitate**. At the same time, the water turns blue from the copper nitrate dissolved in it.

Safety First

Displacement reactions can give off heat, so be careful when handling reactions like these.

They can also produce hydrogen, which is a **flammable** gas.

Reactions in batteries

Have you ever used a battery to make a toy or a flashlight work? Displacement reactions are very important in batteries. **In fact, all batteries depend on chemical reactions to produce electricity.** A chemical reaction occurs when two chemicals react together to form new chemicals.

In batteries, metal rods are surrounded by an acid or a base. As the metal reacts with the acid or base, a stream of tiny particles called **electrons** is produced. This stream of electrons is the electricity.

There are many different types of batteries. The main differences are in the kinds of chemicals used in the battery. Here are the metals used in the main types of batteries:

- Common household batteries use zinc.
- Lithium batteries contain the metal lithium.
- Car batteries have lead plates. This is why car batteries are so heavy!

These are just some of the many different types of batteries.

Electroplating breaks down metal compounds.

ELECTROPLATING

A process called **electroplating** is used to make gold or silver jewelry. Gold or silver compounds are dissolved in water. The metal compound breaks down into **ions**. Ions are particles that have a charge. The charge could be positive or negative. Items made of cheaper metals such as lead and copper are hung in the solution and attached to an **electric circuit**. When electricity flows through the item, the metal **ions** are attracted to the item. They stick to its surface, covering the cheaper metal with a layer of gold or silver.

Oxidation Reactions

When iron combines with oxygen from the air, rust is formed. **The reaction of a substance with oxygen is called oxidation.** Rust is the chemical, iron oxide.

This is the **formula equation** for what happens:

$$2Fe + O_2 \rightarrow 2FeO$$

iron   +   oxygen   →   iron oxide

As rust forms on the iron, chunks of rust flake away and expose the metal underneath. Eventually, the entire object will turn into rust. However, the above reaction is just one of several possible reactions that produce rust.

This old car is covered with rust.

The Statue of Liberty

The Statue of Liberty is made of copper. So, why is she green? Her greenish color is copper carbonate. When copper combines with carbon dioxide, copper carbonate is formed. This carbonate does not flake off like iron oxide. It forms a greenish coating and protects the metal underneath.

TRY THIS! Could you clean the Statue of Liberty?

- Find two or three dirty looking copper pennies.

- Pour a small amount of vinegar in a bowl and shake in about a teaspoon of salt.

- Hold one of the pennies half in the solution and wait a few seconds.

What happens? Do you know why? The dark coating on the penny is mostly copper oxide. The vinegar and salt dissolve the oxide, leaving the copper shiny and clean. You could use the same method to clean the Statue of Liberty!

Protecting pipelines

Can we protect the metal of iron pipelines from reacting and rusting away? Engineers use the activity series to help them. When an iron or steel pipe is placed underground, a piece of magnesium is buried nearby and connected to the pipe with a wire. **Magnesium is a more reactive metal than iron, so it displaces the iron in a reaction.** The piece of magnesium gradually disappears, but the iron pipe remains strong.

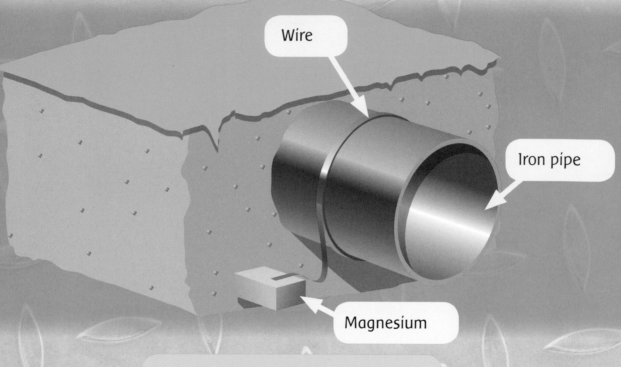

Wire

Iron pipe

Magnesium

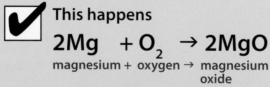

✔ This happens

$$2Mg + O_2 \rightarrow 2MgO$$

magnesium + oxygen → magnesium oxide

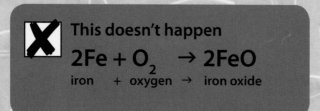

✗ This doesn't happen

$$2Fe + O_2 \rightarrow 2FeO$$

iron + oxygen → iron oxide

Protecting ships

Another way of protecting metals is to coat them with another metal. This is called **galvanizing**. You will read more about this on the next page. Ships use this method so they don't rust away. Magnesium plates are connected to the steel hull of the ship. The magnesium takes the place of the iron in the oxidation reaction, so the hull stays strong. The magnesium slowly fades away, but can be replaced with a new piece.

A magnesium plate is placed on the hull of a ship.

Galvanizing

As you've just read, galvanizing is a way of protecting metals by coating them with another metal. Iron or steel can be covered with zinc, a more reactive metal. One method is to dip the iron or steel item into molten zinc. Another method uses a process called **electroplating**. This produces galvanized iron. The zinc will react with oxygen and carbon in the air, but the zinc oxide that forms makes a tight coating that prevents moisture and air from reaching the iron. Galvanized screws or nails are often used in building fences or putting shingles on a roof.

Galvanized nails

Coating metal

Metal structures can be protected by applying paint or grease. These methods are not as effective as galvanization because only a little crack or spot without paint will quickly begin to rust.

Metal parts may be shipped from the factory covered in grease. When a person is ready to install the part, the grease is cleaned off.

Dissolving Metals

Metallic compounds react in different ways, depending on the metal contained in the compound. Some metallic salts dissolve in water. Others will not dissolve; they are **insoluble**. Knowing the difference can help us separate the metallic salts.

Do they dissolve?

Compounds differ in the amount that will dissolve in water. Some compounds will dissolve easily, while others will not dissolve at all. Silver nitrate will dissolve in water. If hydrochloric acid is added to the solution, silver chloride forms. The silver chloride comes out of the solution as a white solid, the **precipitate**. It does not dissolve in water.

$$AgNO_3 + HCl \rightarrow AgCl + HNO_3$$

silver nitrate + hydrochloric acid → silver chloride (white precipitate) + nitric acid

The solid silver chloride can be removed from the solution using a filter, a mesh with tiny holes. The solution left behind will contain nitric acid, HNO_3.

One use of this process is to purify water. Chemicals are added that will make impurities precipitate out of the water. The impurities are caught in a filter and the pure water is left.

What color is the precipitate in this photo?

Carbonates

Compounds called carbonates have a combination of carbon atoms and oxygen atoms (C and O). Carbonates formed with metals like lithium, sodium, and potassium are fairly **soluble** in water. But the carbonates of beryllium, magnesium, and calcium are insoluble in water.

A chemical similar to carbonate sits on most kitchen shelves. Sodium bicarbonate, $NaHCO_3$, is commonly known as baking soda. You can react this metallic salt with vinegar, which is a weak acid. You will see the reaction form bubbles of a gas.

$$NaHCO_3 + HC_2H_3O_2 \rightarrow Na\,C_2H_3O_2 + H_2O + CO_2$$

| sodium bicarbonate | + acetic acid (ethanoic acid) | → | sodium acetate | + water | + carbon dioxide (gas) |

If the gas from this reaction is tested with a burning splint, the splint will quickly go out. It doesn't pop like hydrogen does or burn quickly like oxygen. This means the gas is carbon dioxide.

DO IT YOURSELF!

Put a spoonful of baking soda in a clear glass. Pour a small amount of vinegar on it. What happens? Can you see the reaction happening? The vinegar and sodium bicarbonate react and the mixture bubbles because carbon dioxide is one of the products.

This is limescale inside of a pipe.

Hard water

Have you ever seen a hard scaly material around a kettle, or faucets? **The scale is called limescale. It is made of calcium carbonate.** Both magnesium and calcium carbonate do not dissolve in water. So they precipitate out of the water and form scale.

Water that contains some magnesium and calcium compounds is called hard water. The magnesium and calcium ions combine with the soap to make a compound that does not dissolve in water. This compound sticks to the sides of the tub. The salts of magnesium and calcium are the soap scum left around a bathtub if hard water is present.

Water softeners

A water softener works to solve this problem. The water is run through beads that have been soaked in sodium chloride. As the hard water passes through the beads, the magnesium and calcium ions are replaced with sodium ions. This stops the limescale from forming. The sodium salts are soluble, so no ring will form around the bathtub. This displacement reaction solves the problem of hard water.

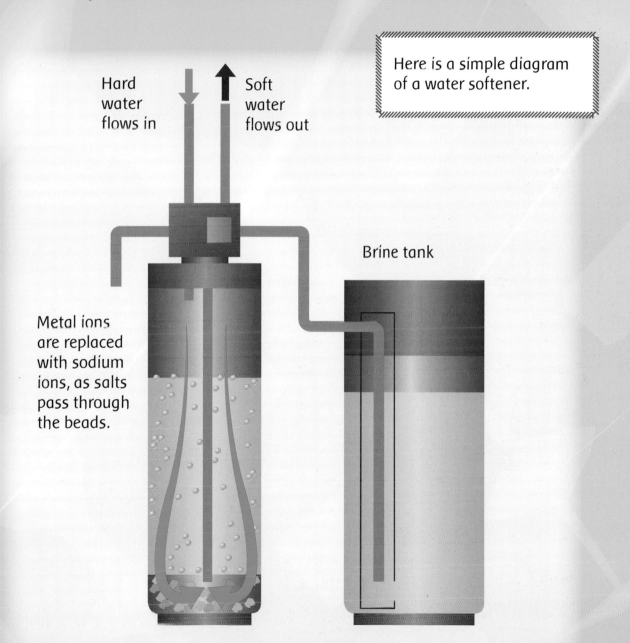

Hard water flows in

Soft water flows out

Here is a simple diagram of a water softener.

Brine tank

Metal ions are replaced with sodium ions, as salts pass through the beads.

Alloys

Metals are amazing. They can mix with other elements to form alloys. <u>Alloys are mixtures of elements, one of which is a metal.</u> The elements do not react with each other.

In general, alloys are stronger or less reactive than the original metals. For example, iron is a soft metal and can be bent or dented. However, when iron is melted with other elements such as nickel or carbon, the result is a strong alloy called steel. Many alloys rust less than the metals they are made from. For example, a fork made of iron or steel would rust quickly. But a stainless steel fork has chromium and nickel added to the metal. Because of this, the fork does not corrode, or become eaten away by chemicals.

A huge factory rolls out sheets of the alloy steel.

Alloys

One of the most common alloys is steel, but there are many others, some of which are shown in the table below.

Alloys	Amounts	Qualities	Uses
carbon steel	0.15 to 0.4% carbon	strong, easily worked	buildings
nickel steel	3.5% nickel	hard, tough	drills, armor plate
stainless steel	18% chromium, 8% nickel	hard, resists corrosion	surgical instruments, eating utensils
brass	67% copper, 33% zinc	shiny, resists corrosion	musical instruments
bronze	90% copper, 10% tin	shiny, fairly strong	decoration
Duralumin	95% aluminum, 4% copper, 0.5% magnesium, 0.5% manganese	very strong, lightweight, resists corrosion	aircraft engines, ships
white gold	75% gold, 3.5% copper, 16.5% nickel, 5% zinc	shiny, good color	jewelry
12-karat gold	50% gold, 50% copper	hard, shiny	jewelry

Each type of steel has a different strength, melting point, and corrosion resistance.

- One of the most common steels is iron mixed with a small amount of carbon. It is used for beams for buildings, bridges, and railroads.
- Nickel steel is useful for making tools because it is stronger than iron alone and keeps a sharp edge.
- Stainless steel is used to make forks and spoons, as well as surgical instruments, because it is very hard and resistant to corrosion.

These musical instruments are made from brass.

Brass

Another familiar alloy is brass. **Brass is an alloy of copper and zinc,** and is used for decorations such as lamp bases and bathroom faucets. Musical instruments such as tubas and trombones are made from brass. The combination of copper and zinc is corrosion resistant and has an attractive golden color when polished.

Making fighter planes and airliners

The aluminum used for plane bodies is an alloy, usually made of 5 percent magnesium. The added magnesium doesn't make the metal heavier, but it provides better strength. It is also resistant to corrosion.

Metals that have memories?

Shape memory alloys are interesting metals. These alloys are usually copper-zinc-aluminum-nickel, copper-aluminum-nickel, or nickel-titanium. The metals can be twisted into a different shape, but the structure of the atoms forces the metal back into its original shape. The metal remembers the shape it should be! Memory metals are used as braces for teeth, eyeglasses, and some airplane engine parts.

These eyeglasses are made of memory metals! Even after they are bent, they retain their shape.

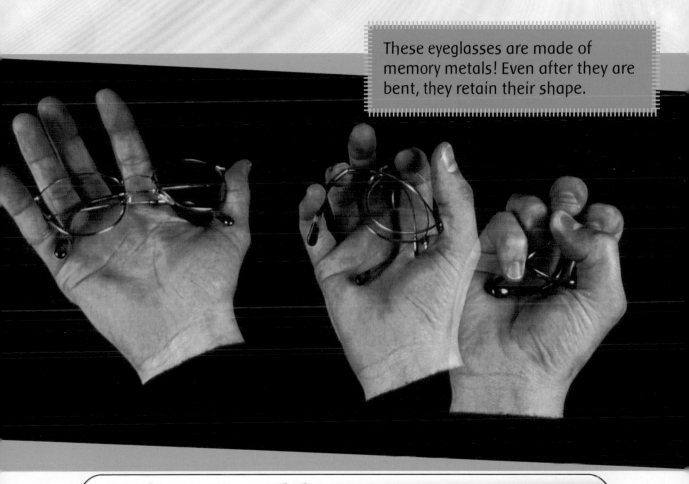

24-karat gold

Pure gold is very soft, so other metals are added to strengthen the gold while keeping the gold color. **Alloys of gold are measured using units called karats**. Gold of 24 karats is 99.9 percent gold or better. Gold of 14 karats has 14 parts gold and 10 parts of another metal. This other metal is usually copper or silver.

Harming the Environment

Did You Know?

Gold can sometimes be found as gold nuggets or layers of gold in rock.

Most metals react easily, so they are found naturally as compounds. **Many metal compounds are found in rocks called ores, which are rocks from the earth that contain metals.** Getting the metals from the ores (extracting it) can be harmful to the environment. Cutting out the rock can destroy plants and homes of animals and insects.

Removing the metals

First, the rock is crushed and treated with chemicals to remove the metal compounds. If pure metal is needed, other reactions are carried out to release the metal. Mercury forms an alloy with other metals very easily, so it is used to pull gold and silver out of their ores. Once the gold is in the mercury, the mixture is heated. The heat turns the mercury into a gas and the gold is left behind. The mercury is captured, cooled back into a liquid, and used again.

Pollution!

Mining metal ores can cause pollution. Gold mines often use poisonous cyanide compounds to extract the gold. The solutions are pumped into holding ponds, but the ponds do not always work. In 1992 a pond at a gold mine in Summitville, Colorado, failed. The poisonous water flowed into a nearby river. Fish and other aquatic wildlife died. The site is now under clean up by the U.S. Superfund program.

Gold mines often use dangerous materials to extract gold. These destroy the environment.

Fish are affected by high levels of mercury. This is very dangerous.

Mercury poisoning

The metal mercury and its compounds can be very poisonous. They can affect people's nervous system and organs. Some mercury occurs naturally in the environment, but power plants and some industries can release mercury compounds into the air. From the air, it travels into waterways and is taken up by fish. In some areas, mercury levels are high enough in fish that the fish should not be eaten. Mercury can cause brain damage and learning disabilities.

Recycling metals

Batteries depend on metals and metal compounds to work. Car batteries contain lead. Other batteries contain nickel, cadmium, and lithium. All these metals can be poisonous to people and animals if they leak into water supplies. So, batteries should always be recycled. Recycling cuts down on waste in landfills and prevents these metals from soaking into our water. Electronics such as computers and televisions also contain poisonous metals. They should also be recycled. Some companies have programs to accept old electronics. They can handle the recycling safely.

Electronics can contain poisonous metals. They must be disposed of properly.

METALS IN THE HUMAN BODY

Many metals and their compounds are necessary for life. The diagram below shows some of these metals and compounds.

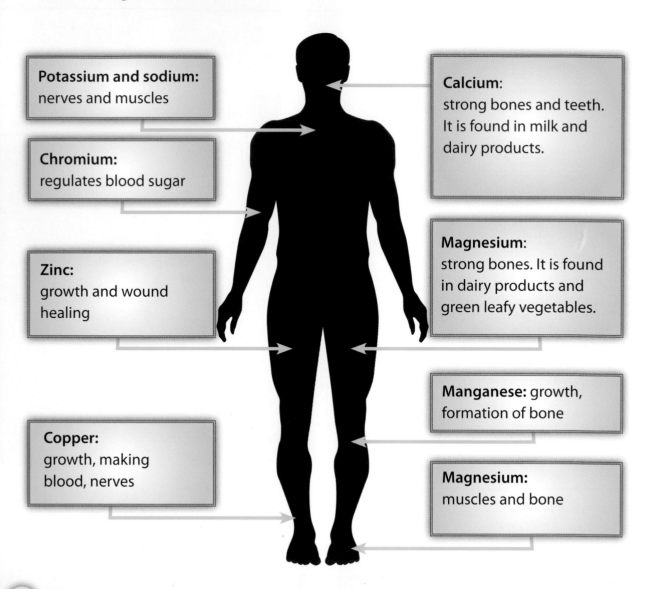

Potassium and sodium: nerves and muscles

Chromium: regulates blood sugar

Zinc: growth and wound healing

Copper: growth, making blood, nerves

Calcium: strong bones and teeth. It is found in milk and dairy products.

Magnesium: strong bones. It is found in dairy products and green leafy vegetables.

Manganese: growth, formation of bone

Magnesium: muscles and bone

Iron

Iron is required by the circulatory system. **Iron helps the red blood cells transport oxygen from the lungs to the cells of the body and to transport carbon dioxide back to the lungs to be exhaled**. The most common sources of iron are red meats and cereals that have added iron.

Brittle bones

Calcium is essential to building strong bones and teeth. Without enough calcium and magnesium, people tend to develop a disease called osteoporosis. The bones become soft and break easily. If a hip breaks because of brittle bones or an accident, a hip replacement surgery may be performed. A titanium joint replaces the bone joint. If just the femur bone (the thigh bone) is broken, a titanium rod is placed inside the bone until it heals. You can see the titanium rod in the photo above.

Titanium is a good metal to use for broken bones, because it does not react with the body.

Why is iron so important?

Iron helps the red blood cells take oxygen from the lungs to cells all over the body. Four atoms of iron bind to hemoglobin. Hemoglobin is a compound in red blood cells that gives them their red color. When the blood carrying the hemoglobin passes through the lungs, four atoms of oxygen bind to the iron atoms. When the hemoglobin-iron-oxygen compound comes to cells that need oxygen, the compound releases the oxygen to the cells.

Even More Reactions of Metals!

Lithium is the lightest metal and an extremely reactive one. Lithium hydroxide is used on spacecraft to make the air pure. The lithium hydroxide absorbs carbon dioxide that is breathed out by humans, removing it from the air.

Magnesium burns not only in oxygen, but also in carbon dioxide. For this reason, a magnesium fire cannot be put out with normal fire extinguishers. Usually, magnesium fires are smothered with dirt.

A compound called thermite results from a reaction of aluminum powder and iron oxide. Thermite can be used to weld train tracks together. The particles of aluminum are ground to a fine powder so that they will react quickly with the iron oxide. The products are aluminum oxide and iron and a lot of heat. The heat melts the iron, which flows into the space of the two tracks and welds them together.

More water reactions:

Calcium is a less reactive metal than sodium or potassium, so it will react slowly with water.

The metals from magnesium to zinc on the activity series will only react with pure water if the water is in the form of steam.

The rest of metals do not react with pure water.

Many metal compounds are colored. Copper salts are blue or green, chromium is yellow, and manganese is violet. These compounds are often used in paints. Some paints even carry colors referring to metals, such as cobalt blue or chrome yellow.

Beryllium-copper alloy is used near rocket fuel, because it won't give off sparks when it is struck.

A beryllium-copper alloy is unique in that it does not give off sparks when struck. It is used for electrical contacts and hammers in explosive places, such as near rocket fuel or flammable gases.

Beryllium-copper alloy

Timeline

6000 BCE TO 750 CE	Known metals include gold, silver, copper, tin, iron, mercury, and lead.
1200s	The metal arsenic is discovered. It was probably isolated from an ore containing arsenic and early people found that it was extremely poisonous.
1500s	Platinum is discovered in the New World by Spanish explorer Antonio de Ulloa. It is usually found in ores that also contain gold.
1700s	Several more metals are discovered including cobalt, nickel, manganese, molybdenum, and tungsten. Scientists isolated these metals from ores, usually by heating the ore and then adding chemicals. Many new elements were discovered this way.
1807	Sir Humphry Davy isolates potassium and sodium as the elemental metal; soon after he also isolates strontium. Davy discovered these elements by separating metal salts using electricity.
1825	Christian Oerstad produces elemental aluminum. The metal was familiar to scientists as a component of a medicine known as alum, but no one had been able to isolate the elemental metal. Oerstad worked out a process to produce elemental aluminum.
1830	Scientists first use electroplating to put a layer of metal over another metal.
1895	X-rays are discovered by German scientist Wilhelm Roentgen; it was the first indication of radioactive elements, as x-rays occur from radioactive decay.
1898	Marie Curie discovers two elements, radium and polonium, and names radioactivity.
1962	Nickel-titanium (Ni-Ti) alloy with shape memory invented.
1980	Duplex stainless steels that resist oxidation are developed.

QUIZ

1. What is the chart that tells which metals are more active than others?

2. If a compound accepts a hydroxide ion in a chemical reaction, does this form an acid or a base?

3. According to the activity series, does gold react easily?

4. The reaction between an acid and a base is called what?

5. What happens in a displacement reaction?

6. What is the reaction of a substance with oxygen called?

7. What are alloys?

8. Why is titanium a good metal to use in the body?

9. What is the lightest metal?

10. Which is your favorite metal? Why? What does it do?

Answers on page 44!

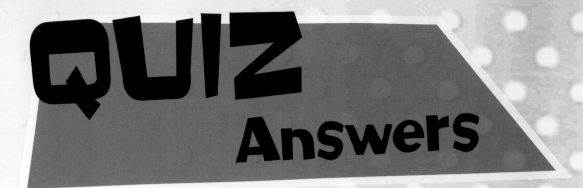

QUIZ Answers

From Page 43

1. The chart is called the activity series.

2. If a compound accepts a hydroxide ion in a chemical reaction, it forms a base.

3. According to the activity series, gold does not react easily.

4. The reaction between an acid and a base is called neutralization.

5. In a displacement reaction, one element displaces another. This means they switch places.

6. The reaction of a substance with oxygen is called oxidation.

7. Alloys are mixtures of elements, one of which is a metal.

8. Titanium does not react with the body, so it is good to use for hip replacement, bone joints, and replacement bones.

9. Lithium is the lightest metal.

10. Answers will vary.

Glossary

Acid A compound that releases a hydrogen ion in a chemical reaction

Activity series A list of metals in order of how easily they react

Alloy Mixture of two or more elements, one of which is a metal

Atom The smallest particle of a chemical element that still has the properties of that element. Atoms are considered the "building blocks" of matter.

Base A compound that accepts a hydrogen ion in a chemical reaction

Chemical reaction Reaction that occurs when two chemicals react together to form new chemicals

Coefficient A number used in a balanced chemical equation to show the relative amount of a reactant or product

Compound Substance that is made up of two or more elements

Concentrated Containing a large amount of solute

Concentration Amount of a substance in a given volume of solution

Conductor A material that allows the easy flow of electricity

Corrode To become eaten away by chemicals. Rusting is a type of corrosion.

Dilute Containing a small amount of solute

Displacement reaction Reaction in which a more reactive element takes the place of a less reactive element in a compound

Dissolve To break down into molecules and mix evenly and completely

Electrical circuit The path of an electrical current along wires

Electron Extremely tiny particle that is part of an atom

Electroplating A process where a layer of metal is put over another metal by using electricity

Element Substance that cannot be split into a simpler substance by a chemical reaction.

Flammable Capable of being easily ignited and of burning quickly

Formula Equation A chemical equation written in chemical symbols, rather than words

Galvanizing A way of protecting metals by coating them with another metal

Insoluble Not able to be dissolved

Ion Atom or group of atoms with an electrical charge

Metal Any element in the periodic table that is shiny and that conducts heat and electricity well. Most metals are also hard.

Molecule Combination of atoms, held together by chemical bonds

Neutralization The reaction between an acid and a base

Ores Rocks from the earth that contain metals

Oxidation Adding oxygen to an element or compound in a reaction. For example, carbon is oxidized when it reacts with oxygen to make carbon dioxide.

Periodic table of elements A table that lists the known elements, organized according to the element's properties

Precipitate Solid that forms in a reaction and that can be filtered out of the solution

Radioactive Something that gives off tiny particles of radiation

Refine To remove impurities from a substance to make it pure

Soluble Able to be dissolved

Further Information

Books to read

Baldwin, Carol. *Material Matters: Metals*. Chicago: Raintree, 2005.

Gardner, Robert. *Chemistry Science Fair Projects : Using Acids, Bases, Metals, Salts and Inorganic Stuff*. Berkeley Heights, NJ: Enslow Publishers, 2004.

Kjelle, Marylou Morano. *The Properties of Metals*. New York: Rosen Publishing, 2006.

Miller, Ron. *The Elements*. Minneapolis, MN: Twenty-First Century Books, 2006.

Oxlade, Chris. *Materials Changes and Reactions*. Chicago: Heinemann Library, 2007.

Parsons, Jayne. *The Way Science Works*. New York: DK Publishing, 2002.

Stille, Darlene R. *Chemical Change: From Fireworks to Rust*. Minneapolis, MN: Compass Point, 2006.

Websites

http://qldscienceteachers.tripod.com/junior/chem/metals.html
Explore the science of metals and their reactions at this fun and colorful site!

http://www.chemsoc.org/viselements/
This highly graphic site allows you to visualize the elements and learn more about the periodic table.

http://jchemed.chem.wisc.edu/JCESOFT/CCA/CCA3/MAIN/METALI2/PAGE1.HTM
You can actually view videos of metals reacting with chemicals at this site!

Look It Up!

Do some more research on one or more of these topics:
- Gold
- Titanium and the human body
- Displacement reactions
- The periodic table of elements

Index